ALSO BY
Rachel Renée Russell

Dork Diaries

Dork Diaries: Party Time

Dork Diaries: Pop Star

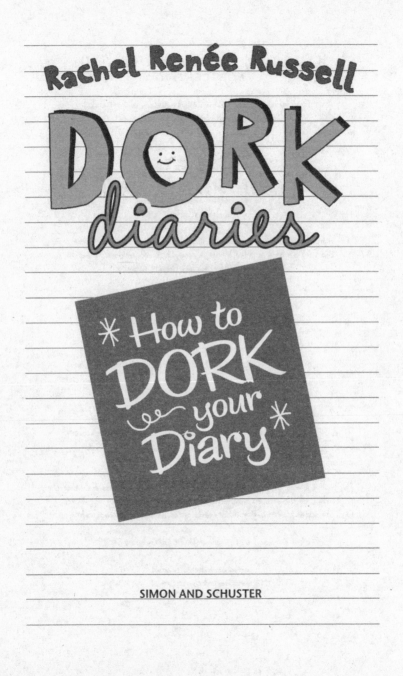

Rachel Renée Russell

DORK
diaries

How to DORK your Diary

SIMON AND SCHUSTER

First published in Great Britain in 2011 by Simon & Schuster UK Ltd
A CBS COMPANY

First published in the USA in 2011 by Aladdin, an imprint of
Simon & Schuster Children's Publishing Division.

5 7 9 10 8 6 4

Simon & Schuster UK Ltd
1st Floor, 222 Gray's Inn Road
London
WC1X 8HB

Simon & Schuster Australia, Sydney
Simon & Schuster India, New Delhi

A CIP catalogue record for this book is available from the British Library.

ISBN 978-0-85707-980-0

Printed and bound by CPI Group (UK) Ltd, Croydon, CR0 4YY

www.simonandschuster.co.uk
www.simonandschuster.com.au
www.dorkdiaries.com

This book is dedicated to YOU,
my wonderful readers!

Fill it with your daydreams,
drama and doodles.
And always remember to let
your inner Dork shine through!

FRIDAY, AT HOME, 6:05 A.M.

<u>OMG!!</u>

I just had the most HORRIFIC nightmare!

The worst in my <u>entire</u> life!

I'm soooo FREAKED OUT I can barely write this.

ME, FREAKING OUT

I'm having cold sweats, my heart is pounding and my brain is . . . numb with such intense . . . anguish it feels like it's about to, um . . . EXPLODE!

WHY?!

I DREAMED I LOST MY DIARY AT SCHOOL ☹!!!!!!!

YES!! At SCHOOL!! Like, how CRAZY is THAT?!

The weird thing is that it seems like it actually happened. Because as soon as I woke up, all these detailed memories came flooding into my head, making me feel even more confused.

I can't imagine NOT writing in my diary! It's like I'm addicted or something.

In my dream I was so desperate that I found Brianna's old doodle book at the bottom of her toy box and started writing in that instead.

But mostly I was FRANTIC that someone would find my diary and read all the SUPERpersonal, SUPERembarrassing, SUPERsecret stuff about

3

Me and ~~the~~ Princess
Sugar Plum kissing all
the ~~cute~~ cute Baby unicorns

~~Me~~ Me

By "a"
Brianna

AAAHHH!!

That was me screaming.

WHY?

Because if I'm writing in BRIANNA'S DOODLE BOOK, that can mean only one thing . . .

I LOST MY DIARY AT SCHOOL YESTERDAY ☹!!

AAAHHH!!!

I think I may be having a nervous breakdown or something because suddenly I just started crying and couldn't stop.

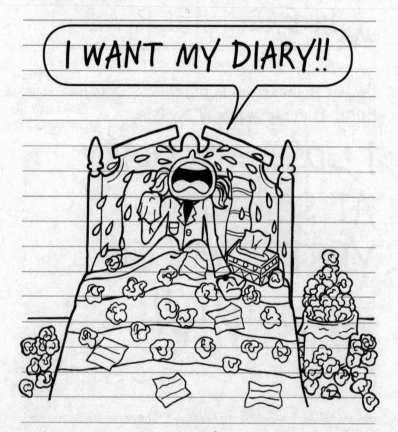

My room was a total mess after just one box of tissues.

But by the time I sobbed my way through seven boxes of tissues, I looked like a giant piece of FLUFF.

With EYEBALLS!

PLEASE. HELP. ME.

ME, BURIED BENEATH A HUGE MOUNTAIN OF 2,184 WADDED TISSUES

As much as I wanted to just lie there staring at the wall and sulking, I FINALLY decided it was time to drag my butt out of bed.

7

WHY?

Because all those wet, soggy tissues were quickly starting to dry and harden around my body, potentially transforming ME into a HUMAN piñata!!

And Brianna just LOVES piñatas.

I was absolutely TERRIFIED she would:

1. Dump lots of sweets down my throat.

2. String me up on a pole.

3. Hit me with a plastic bat until I either burst or coughed up some sweets.

That child has serious issues.

I'm just saying. . . . ☹!!

AT HOME, 6:30 A.M.

I can't believe this is actually happening to me!

The last time I remember seeing my diary was yesterday at breakfast.

After I finished writing in it, I stuck it inside that cute little front pocket of my backpack just like I always do.

I had a vocabulary quiz in French and a chapter test in geometry, so I didn't have time to write in it until my final class.

And when I opened the front pocket of my backpack, my diary was GONE ☹!!!

Being the biggest dork in the entire school is bad enough. And now everyone is going to be reading my diary!

I'm WORSE than a TOTAL LOSER!!! I'm a

Okay! Is it just ME, or are these drawings a desperate cry for help?!

Brianna needs to be placed on a very potent antipsychotic medication. ASAP!

I'm just sayin'. . . !

✳ PLAN FOR FINDING MY LOST DIARY ✳

Step 1. Check the lost and found in school office. (If not found, proceed to Step 2)

Step 2. Check each of my classrooms. (If not found, proceed to Step 3)

Step 3. Check hallways, cafeteria and library. (If STILL not found, proceed to Step 4)

Step 4. Crawl inside my locker, slam the door shut, and . . . **DIE** ☹**!!**

ME→

HERB, THE JANITOR, DISCOVERS WHAT'S CAUSING
THE STINK COMING FROM LOCKER #724

This whole fiasco is SO massively TRAUMATIZING I can barely think straight.

I'm sure I'm probably suffering from some very horrible and rare disorder like, um, Stress-Related Brain . . . Constipation!

And my illness will make it nearly impossible for me to keep a diary.

At this point, the only thing I can do is use Brianna's doodle book to write very specific instructions to myself about HOW to keep a diary.

The good news is that anyone can use my personal tips to make their own diary.

Learning how to dork a diary will be both a thrilling and rewarding experience for all humankind.

And who knows, maybe one day your diary could even save your life. . .

14

See what I mean?!

AM I NOT BRILLIANT ☺?!!

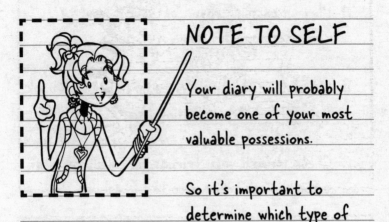

NOTE TO SELF

Your diary will probably become one of your most valuable possessions.

So it's important to determine which type of diary is best suited for your personality.

HOW TO DORK YOUR DIARY TIP #1

DISCOVER YOUR DIARY IDENTITY.

Answer the following questions to find out the best type of diary for you.

1. It's a Saturday afternoon. Your homework is all done and you have an hour to do whatever you want. You decide to:

   A. Play an exciting round of your favourite computer or video game.

   B. Spend time relaxing by reading that new book your BFF has been raving about.

   C. Check in with your friends via email, text, or a social-networking site like Facebook.

   D. Let your creative juices flow by drawing your favourite anime characters.

2. You left your diary in your English class, and your secret crush returns it to you during lunch. You:

   A. Email him one of those cute animated thank you e-cards and surprise him with his fave chocolate bar as a reward!

B. Gag on your lunch and then rush to the girls' toilets, where you spend the rest of the day hiding out in a locked cubicle.

C. Hope he read the part in your diary about you liking him, so he'll *finally* ask you to the school dance. Hey, it's only a week away!

D. Blush profusely when he compliments that funky self-portrait in glitter you're working on for the art show and offer to draw a zany caricature of him as a thank you.

3. When something is really bothering you, you usually:

A. Ponder the problem for an hour or two and then try to forget about it by doing a self-induced brain freeze with three tubs of Ben & Jerry's Chunky Monkey ice cream.

B. Privately obsess over the problem all day long while trying to convince everyone who asks "Are you okay?" that you're fine and nothing is bothering you because (1) your problem is way too complicated for them to understand, and (2) you're way too exhausted from pretending you're just fine to explain it to them.

C. Vent about the problem rather loudly to anyone and everyone who'll listen to you. Because if YOU ain't happy, NOBODY should be happy!

D. Distract yourself from worrying by channelling all that negative energy into a creative project. Like painting a still-life mural inside your locker and adding a water fountain, scented candles and a yoga mat, and then totally chilling out in between classes.

4. Your birthday was three months ago and you still need to send your grandma a thank you note for that hideous avocado-green sweater she knitted for you that was two sizes too big and more itchy than a severe case of fleas. You:

A. Drop her a quick email sincerely telling her how you'll cherish her gift forever, while casually mentioning how much you really, really LOVE gift cards because one size fits all and they don't usually cause a rash.

B. Compose a heartfelt, handwritten thank you note informing her that her gift is being worn almost daily. But leave out the part about how you buried it out in the garden and your dad accidentally found it when he was watering the grass and now it's his lucky bowling sweater.

C. Friend your grandma online and then post your thank you note on her page along with a picture of yourself in the sweater SHE knitted so that her fourteen online friends can see it. But also wear the ski mask YOU knitted so that your 1,784 online friends won't recognize you in a sweater that looks like dirty yak fur.

D. Paint a life-size portrait of yourself wearing the sweater and send it to your grandma to show your gratitude. Because thanks to her, some very lucky dog or cat at the local animal shelter will give birth to her litter on a warm, fuzzy, two-sizes-too-big avocado-green sweater.

5. Which of the following is most true?

A. You're a very tech-savvy person. You're a team
   player and always up for a challenge.

B. You're friendly and a hopeless romantic.
   You love curling up in a comfy blanket and
   daydreaming.

C. You're happy and have lots of friends.
   There's always some type of drama going
   on in your life.

D. You're creative and enjoy art, music, drama and poetry. Your personal style is unique and slightly edgy.

6. You hear the news that your BFF's football team just won the regional championship. You:

A. Send her the text message "You GO, GIRL! Congrats!"

B. Congratulate her with a big hug when you see her.

C. Leave her a phone message of you screaming hysterically.

D. Surprise her with a handmade poster on her locker that says "Congrats! You ROCK!"

7. You're about to wash your favourite pair of jeans and find ten dollars stashed in the back pocket from your last babysitting job. You're RICH! So you treat yourself to:

A. A ticket to that blockbuster movie based on your favourite book. You've been waiting, like, FOREVER for it to come out!

B. Gourmet CUPCAKES! SQUEEEEEEE!!

C. Lip gloss! There's a buy-two-get-one-FREE sale at the mall!

D. Music for your iPod. There are some new tunes you've heard lately that are real ear candy.

8. You're at a sleepover and it's game time. Which of the following would you rather play?

A. Just Dance on the Wii

B. The Game of Life

C. Truth or Dare

D. Pictionary

Now look back at which answer you circled for each question.

Which letter do you have the most of?

I have mostly _____.

MOSTLY As
You are smart and curious, and you like learning new things. You will most enjoy keeping a diary on your computer. Write detailed entries about your interesting adventures and new discoveries.

MOSTLY Bs
You are kind and sensitive, and you like helping others. You will most enjoy writing in a diary or journal. Your dreams and feelings are sacred. Share them with your diary like a best friend.

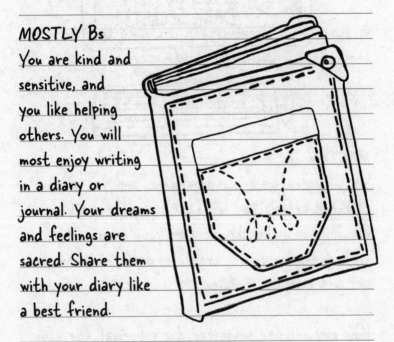

MOSTLY Cs
You are friendly and outgoing, and you love people. You will most enjoy writing a blog. Select a fab online ID and share your exciting, DIVALICIOUS life with your friends.

MOSTLY Ds

You are creative and independent, and you are a talented artist. You will most enjoy keeping your thoughts in a sketchbook. Let your innermost feelings inspire you to create emo poetry, beautiful art and hilarious doodles.

Now try out the suggested diary format for your personality. If you love it, you've found your match! However, if it's not the best fit, try the others and select the one you're most comfortable with. GOOD LUCK ☺!

I'm already dreading school today.

Part of me wants to just give up and go back to bed. But since I desperately need to find my diary, staying home is NOT an option.

Just the thought of kids at my school reading my diary makes me physically ill. I was so nauseated this morning, I could barely even eat anything.

Of course, it didn't help that Brianna was making a huge gourmet breakfast for Miss Penelope.

SORRY! But Miss Penelope is JUST a stupid little HAND PUPPET! Any IDIOT could take one look at her and know she could NEVER eat that much food!!

But more than anything, I was totally GROSSED OUT by the nasty mess Brianna was making.

MISS PENELOPE SAYS, "YUMMY!!"

ME, TRYING REALLY HARD *NOT* TO THROW UP IN MY MOUTH!

Why, why, why was I not born an only child ☹?!!

NOTE TO SELF

It's always fun to write about things that make you happy. But did you know that writing about a bad experience or disappointment can sometimes make you feel a lot better about the situation? If you're having a really cruddy day, remember to use your diary as a way to help you vent and work through your frustrations.

WRITE ABOUT THE GOOD, THE BAD AND THE UGLY.

THE GOOD:

Me, the day I won first place in our school art show!!

29

Tuesday 10/3/15

Write about the BEST thing that has ever happened to you. How did you feel?

In school I got 100% In My comprehension exam. I was over the Moon.

Draw a picture: _____

THE BEST THING
THAT EVER HAPPENED TO ME ☺!

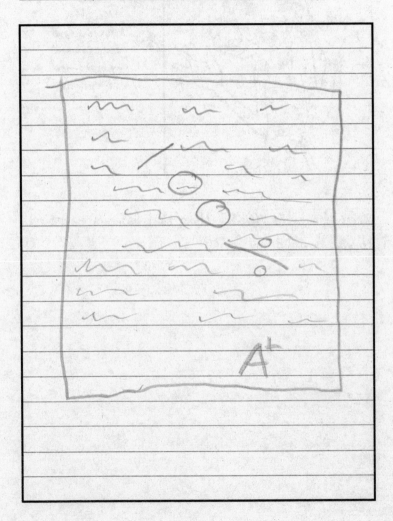

THE BAD:

Me, after MacKenzie and Jessica ruined my brand-new party dress!

Write about the WORST thing that has ever happened to you. How did you feel?

My Parents Split up
I was devastated

Draw a picture:

THE WORST THING
THAT EVER HAPPENED TO ME ☹!

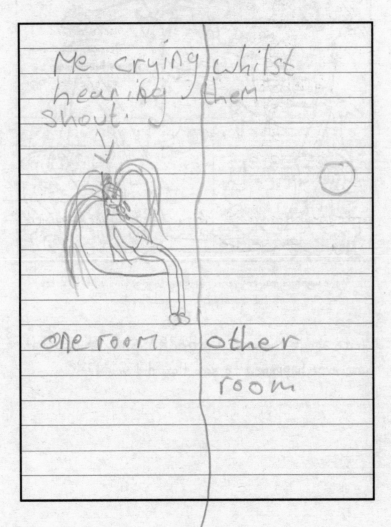

Me crying whilst hearing them shout

one room | other room

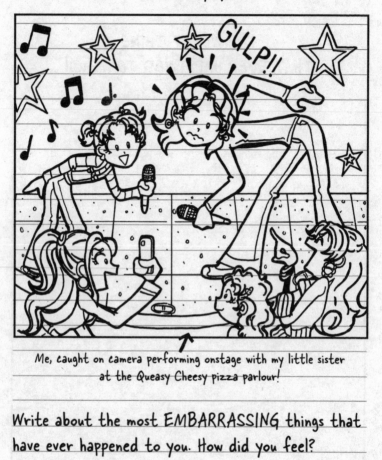

Me, caught on camera performing onstage with my little sister at the Queasy Cheesy pizza parlour!

Write about the most EMBARRASSING things that have ever happened to you. How did you feel?

Draw pictures:

THE TWO MOST EMBARRASSING THINGS THAT EVER HAPPENED TO ME 😣!

NOTE TO SELF

Make sure you write in
your diary every single day.
Even if you LOSE your
diary, just keep writing
in a spare notebook or in
your little sister's annoying

37

ME AND MISS ~~PEAL~~ ~~PENELO~~
PENELOPE

SLURP ICE CREAM

doodle book.   BY ~~BRA~~ BRIANNA

38

ALWAYS DO THE WRITE THING.

Surprise! This is a POP QUIZ! Grab a pencil or pen and write a diary entry RIGHT NOW about what happened to you today! Keep writing until you see the word "STOP".

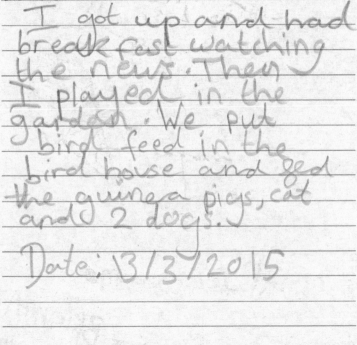

I got up and had breakfast watching the news. Then I played in the garden. We put bird feed in the bird house and fed the guinea pigs, cat and 2 dogs.

Date: 13/3/2015

Then I did
homework - ughh! 🙂 -
and was text-
ing some of my BFFS
for ages. After
that I watched
a ✗ Movie. Then
had supper. Then
a bath. Then
~~stuf~~ BED 😴 ᶻᶻᶻᶻ

ᶻᶻᶻ

As soon as I got to school, I practically ran to the office. I didn't even wait around for my BFFs, Chloe and Zoey.

The school secretary, Mrs Pearson, was putting mail in the teacher mailboxes.

"Um . . . excuse me, but has anyone found a lost book?" I asked frantically.

"Good morning, Nikki. Actually, a student DID turn in a book yesterday! He said he found it in the hall near the cafeteria."

I could not believe my luck! I was so happy and relieved, I could have hugged her.

"OMG! Someone found it and turned it in?" I squealed excitedly. "I'm pretty sure it's MINE!"

Thank goodness this nightmare was finally over.

When Mrs Pearson handed me the book, I took one look and my heart dropped.

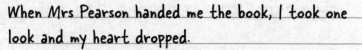

It was NOT my diary!

I needed ANOTHER geometry book like I needed a hole in the head. I didn't understand the maths problems in the book I already had!

"Um, thanks. But this ISN'T my book," I muttered, and handed it back to Mrs Pearson.

"Well, take a look in the lost and found box. There's a chance it could be in there," she said encouragingly.

I closed my eyes and prayed it would be there.

Please let my diary be in the lost and found!

Please let my diary be in the lost and found!

Please let my diary be in the lost and found!

Then I sighed and walked over to a large cardboard box sitting in a corner.

I slowly opened it and carefully went through each and every item. . .

ME, SEARCHING FOR MY DIARY
AMONG ALL THE VERY WEIRD ITEMS IN
THE LOST AND FOUND

Princess Sugar Plum lunch box

Flea collar

Pet lizard

LOST 'N' FOUND

Chewed pencil

Mouldy sandwich

3-D glasses

Retainer

Matted hair extension

But unfortunately, it was NOT in there.

I bit my lip and tried to blink back my tears.

"Don't worry, dear. It's bound to turn up later today," Mrs Pearson said, trying to make me feel better. "And to make sure we find it, I'm going to post a note alerting all my student office assistants to keep an eye out for a book belonging to Nikki Maxwell! Okay?"

That's when my knees got weak and my stomach felt so queasy I thought I was going to throw up.

But it WASN'T because of the mouldy sandwich.

Or the dirty retainer.

Or the matted hair extension (which was quite disgusting in a peculiar sort of way).

I suddenly realized my little diary problem was probably going to get a lot WORSE before it got better.

WHY?!

Because JESSICA HUNTER is a student OFFICE ASSISTANT!

And Jessica's BFF is MACKENZIE HOLLISTER!

And everyone knows that MacKenzie Hollister

HATES MY GUTS!!

Even if at some point my diary IS turned in to the lost and found, there's a VERY good chance MacKenzie is going to intercept it, read it and then plaster pages around the school — just to make my life more miserable than it already is. And there's nothing I can do about it.

Except rush straight to the girls' toilets and have a massive mental meltdown. . .

AAAAAAAHHH☹!!

(That was me screaming. AGAIN!)

NOTE TO SELF
WARNING:

Unfortunately, parents, bratty kid sisters and brothers, friends, enemies and even total strangers LOVE to read diaries that do NOT belong to them.

HOW TO DORK YOUR DIARY TIP #4

NEVER, EVER LEAVE YOUR DIARY WHERE A NOSY CREEP CAN SNEAK A PEEK!

OMG, NIKKI! YOU'RE WRITING IN A DIARY? CAN I READ IT?

OH, THIS? IT'S JUST A . . . BOOK I GOT FROM MY DOCTOR ON, UM . . . TOENAIL ODOUR.

If someone caught you writing in your diary, what would you say to trick them? Write four different responses below:

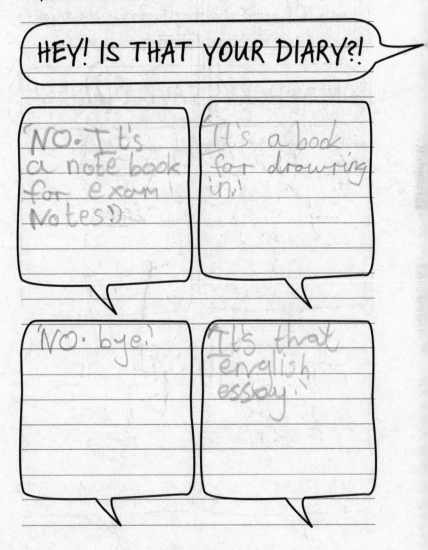

HEY! IS THAT YOUR DIARY?!

'NO. It's a note book for exam Notes!)'

'It's a book for drawing in.'

'NO. bye.'

'It's that english essay.'

Never let anyone tell you that keeping a diary is a silly or childish thing to do. Reflecting on your feelings and experiences is actually a very mature activity. If someone said something rude about you having a diary, what would your response be?

ONLY DORKS HAVE DIARIES!

NO. The only one who is a dork is the one sayin' it.

SO IF taylor swift had a diary she'd be a dork?

OH Yeah ?!

GET LOST

How would you disguise your diary? Draw phoney book covers on the next two pages:

PHONEY BOOK COVER #1

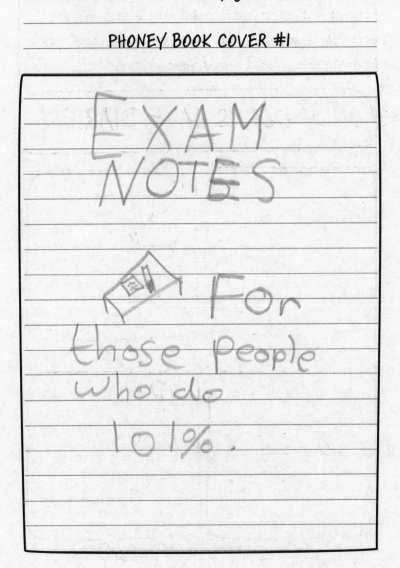

EXAM NOTES

For those people who do 101%.

ENGLISH CLASS, 8:00 A.M.

I was completely out of breath by the time I arrived at my first class.

I frantically checked around my desk, on the counters and on the bookshelves. But there was no sign of my diary ☹! I was like, JUST GREAT!

I collapsed into my seat, closed my eyes and massaged my temples, trying to replay yesterday's events in my mind.

If I had somehow lost my diary, WHO would have been around me to find it? I suspiciously eyeballed all the potential suspects in my classroom.

That's when I remembered that Chloe walked with me to class yesterday. As usual, she was raving nonstop about the latest novel she'd just finished. It was called . . .

"OMG, Nikki! It is the BEST book EVER! I could NOT stop reading it.

"This talented artist is obsessed with drawing this supercute guy she has made up in her mind. Then one day he shows up at her school as a new student. And he can read her thoughts.

"The doodle dude seems really nice until her crush, Hunk Finn, an even cuter guy in her art class, sketches her for a class project and shares a double-fudge chocolate cupcake with her.

"When Doodle Dude starts acting scary jealous, the artist decides she has no choice but to secretly erase all her drawings to get rid of him.

"Then she totally freaks out when Doodle Dude steals ALL her rubbers so she can't erase him. And then he starts eating paper to gain superpowers and immortality.

"Nikki, since you're an artist too, I think you're gonna LOVE it!"

I was like, "Um, thanks, Chloe. Can't wait!"

Then she handed me her *Deadly Doodle Dude* book, and I unzipped my backpack and stuck it inside.

That was probably when my diary accidentally fell out. . .

AND CHLOE FOUND
IT ☹?!

I have to admit, Chloe is hopelessly obsessed with romance novels.

And she'll read just about ANYTHING. Soup can labels. Lip gloss tubes.

What if she picked up my DIARY, read it and LOVED, LOVED, LOVED all the wacky drama?!

I know this might sound really crazy. . . ! But what if Chloe actually turned my very private, dorky tales of WOE into a bestselling book series?!

AND a blockbuster Hollywood movie?!

Without even telling me?!!

I'd probably NEVER, EVER get over it. My life would be totally RUINED.

And then, many years later, Chloe and I might just happen to see each other on the street . . .

NIKKI, DAH-LING! I WOULDN'T BE FAMOUS AND FILTHY RICH IF I HADN'T FOUND *YOUR* DIARY. PLEASE, LET ME AT LEAST DROP A QUARTER IN YOUR LITTLE CUP!

WILL WORK FOR FOOD

ME

CHLOE

Hey, it could happen! Why is my life so hopelessly CRUDDY?!

NOTE TO SELF

Keeping a diary isn't just about describing what kind of person you are. It's also about DISCOVERING what kind of person you are.

That's why it's important to dig deep and examine your thoughts and feelings. Be very comfortable writing about YOU!

IT'S ALL ABOUT ME, MYSELF AND I.

If you can answer each and every one of the
following questions, you'll be on your way to keeping
an AWESOME diary.

What makes you really happy?

Me and my
Mum
together.

What makes you really sad?

Sick
people/animals.

What's your biggest life accomplishment?

a Fashion
journalist

What are you most proud of?

getting 100% in an exam

What's your biggest embarrassment?

THE STAGE

my Lines

What's your biggest fear?

being LOst

Who's your biggest hero?

Anne Frank

What do you want to be when you're older?

A journalist

What are three of your favourite TV shows?

Horrid henry

the next step

Sparticle Mystery

What are three of your favourite films?

Frozen

The box trolls

ELF

Who are three of your favourite pop stars?

Beyonce

katy perry

Talor swift

What are three of your favourite books?

Dork Diaries

Hobbit

What are three of your favourite songs?

Lips are Movin

Heroes

1000 Years

What's your favourite food?

SASAUGES

What's your least favourite food?

Baked

Beans

Who's your best friend in the world?

Izzy

M

Who are you hopelessly crushing on?

?

Where do you like to hang out?

The
Park

HELP!! Today is turning into the WORST day EVER!

Right before French class I decided to search all the girls' toilets for my missing diary.

And guess who I ran into?!

HINT: She was looking in the mirror, slathering on seventeen layers of Fluorescent Candy Apple Bliss lip gloss.

You guessed it!

MACKENZIE HOLLISTER!!

And get this! She was actually NICE to me.

Which, of course, made me SUPERsuspicious.

Especially when she bumped into me and then tried to act all innocent and apologetic, like the whole thing was just an accident.

"Oopsie! I just bumped into you, Nikki. But it was totally an accident. Sorry! I hope you'll accept my apology. By the way, does this lip gloss match my shoes?"

I could NOT believe my ears. How dare MacKenzie apologize for being a clumsy ox AND ask me for fashion advice, all in the same breath! Where did that girl learn her manners? Doggie obedience school? I'm just sayin'!

Anyway, as soon as I left the toilets, I noticed everyone in the hall was pointing and laughing at me.

And I didn't have the slightest idea why.

Well,

MacKenzie had given me a little, um, PRESENT...

ME, BEING PUBLICLY HUMILIATED BY
MACKENZIE'S LITTLE PRANK

When I saw her again in French class, I had to
restrain myself from sneaking off to the girls'
toilets to borrow a roll of toilet paper.

WHY?

Because a very dark and evil side of me wanted
to TP her right there in the middle of class.

ME, GIVING MACKENZIE A LITTLE TASTE OF HER OWN MEDICINE!

EVIL ME

Anyway, I was a little surprised when she sashayed over to my desk.

"I heard from a very reliable source that you lost your little diary. It would be horrible if all your secrets got out. So I have some important news for you!"

My mouth dropped open and my heart skipped a beat. OMG!! MacKenzie knew my diary was missing?!

Had she found out from Jessica ALREADY? My worst NIGHTMARE was coming true!

And I had a really bad feeling about her news.

"Actually, MacKenzie, it would be news to me if, for once, you DIDN'T stick YOUR nose in MY personal business."

That's when she stared right at me with her icy blue eyes.

She glared at me, stuck her nose in the air and then sashayed back to her desk.

I just HATE it when MacKenzie sashays!

But now I have just TWO nagging questions:

1. WILL SHE FIND MY DIARY BEFORE I DO?

2. IF SHE DOES, WHAT EVIL, CRUEL AND DIABOLICAL PLAN DOES SHE HAVE IN STORE FOR ME? ☹!!

It's hard to concentrate on my French lesson with MacKenzie eyeballing me all evil-like from across the room.

I swear! That girl is going to be really sorry when

ME AND MAX the ~~ROC#~~ ROACH

GO FOR A WALK

BY

Brianna

71

Did I just see Max the Roach on a . . . LEASH?!

Okay, I give up!

There is no question about it . . .

I'M DOOMED!! ☹!!

NOTE TO SELF

You never know if your diary might fall into the wrong hands. Just in case, make sure you have codes that only YOU understand!

HOW TO DORK YOUR DIARY TIP #6

WHEN NECESSARY, GO INTO SECRET-CODE MODE.

Chloe and Zoey and I always talk about the CCP
(Cute, Cool & Popular) crowd and GGG-ing (giggling,
gossiping and glossing). Make a list of codes you and
your friends have and what they all mean.

Yolo = You only live
once

LoL = Laugh out
loud

kk = Okay

Cbb = can't be bothered

BTW = By the Way

You could also come up with new meanings for these abbreviations and then no one will be able to crack your code!

WCD = Westchester Country Day OR World-Class Dork OR: Worlds classyest dog.

LOL = Laughing Out Loud OR Laughing Obnoxiously Loud OR: Loser of Losers

BRB = Be Right Back OR Busy Rescuing Batman OR:

Bed, rest, Breakcase

BTW = By the Way OR:

But the Work

OMG = Oh My God OR: _Oh Man!_
Gees.

CCP = Cute, Cool & Popular OR:

Cool, classy people

RCS = Roller-Coaster Syndrome OR: _Rovers_
can sting

TTYL = Talk to You Later OR:
Tell the yolo loser

JK = Just Kidding OR: _Jokes kk_

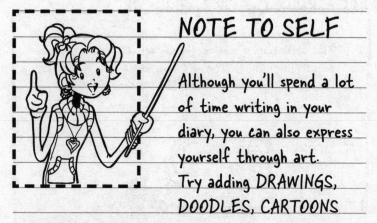

NOTE TO SELF

Although you'll spend a lot of time writing in your diary, you can also express yourself through art. Try adding DRAWINGS, DOODLES, CARTOONS and COMIC STRIPS. They can be serious, artsy, emo, or just plain silly. If you're a supertalented artist, create a masterpiece. Or try drawing simple stick people. Or trace your hand and make it into a turkey like you did back in primary school. Just have FUN!

HOW TO DORK YOUR DIARY TIP #7

RELEASE YOUR INNER ARTIST!

Here is a four-panel comic strip called "My Diary Drama". (A panel is just another name for the box the artwork is placed inside.)

Now you're going to make your own four-panel comic strip! But before you get started, plan what it is going to be about.

My comic strip is called:

~~Hedie Horses~~

Sisters

PANEL 1
Panel 1 will contain a picture of:

Me + my sisters

The characters are saying:

arguing

PANEL 2

Panel 2 will contain a picture of:

us making up

The characters are saying:

being sorry

PANEL 3

Panel 3 will contain a picture of:

us hugging

The characters are saying:

Love yah

PANEL 4

Panel 4 will contain a picture of:

playing

The characters are saying:

weee!

Now you're ready to draw your own comic strip in the space provided. Have fun ☺!

84

I'm beginning to think my situation is HOPELESS!

I've checked all the halls, the library and the cafeteria. AND I just scoured my social studies classroom.

But still no trace of my diary ☹!!

That's when I started wondering if maybe someone picked it up by accident.

Who, other than Chloe, did I come in close contact with yesterday?

Well, that's a no-brainer! The answer is . . . ZOEY!!

As library shelving assistants, Chloe, Zoey and I go to the library during study hall. We gather up all the library books and place them back on their proper shelves.

I have to admit, I don't exactly remember whether

or not I even had my diary in the library yesterday. But what if I DID. . . ?!

OMG! What if Zoey accidentally grabbed my diary while she was gathering that huge stack of books?

← ZOEY ACCIDENTALLY GRABBING MY DIARY!!

And what if while she was putting them back on the shelves, she found my diary and READ IT?! She'd have enough drama to launch her own TV talk show . . .

BACK AGAIN TODAY IS NIKKI, TO SHARE *MORE* ABOUT HER AMAZINGLY PATHETIC LIFE!

Right now I'm so utterly frustrated, I feel like crying.

But mostly I have this very sick feeling deep down in my gut that I'll probably never see my diary again.

I can't believe this is happening to me!

☹!!

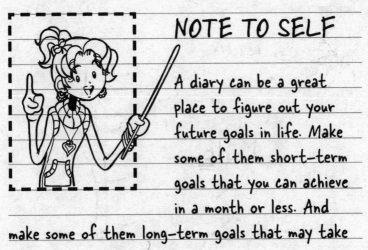

NOTE TO SELF

A diary can be a great place to figure out your future goals in life. Make some of them short-term goals that you can achieve in a month or less. And make some of them long-term goals that may take a year or more to achieve.

Remember to keep track of the ones you've accomplished and set exciting new ones.

HOW TO DORK YOUR DIARY TIP #8

DARE TO DREAM ABOUT YOUR FUTURE!

List three things you'd like to accomplish.

Tomorrow:

A good ~~Ma~~ School Day

Next week:

Fun

Next month:

FUN

Next year:

Horse

Riding

I had barely got out on to the gym floor when both Chloe and Zoey came rushing over.

"Hey, Nikki!" Chloe said, looking a bit worried. "We waited for you by your locker this morning, and again after second period. We started thinking maybe you were at home sick or something."

"Yeah, we're glad to see you," said Zoey. "Although, to be honest, you DO look a little down today. Are you okay?" she asked, giving me a big hug.

I do NOT deserve friends like Chloe and Zoey!

Why did I EVER suspect that my BFFs would find my diary, read it and then share it with the entire world? I could trust them with my LIFE!

A wave of guilt washed over me. That's when I decided to tell Chloe and Zoey what happened.

I lowered my voice to barely a whisper.

ACTUALLY, I AM A LITTLE DOWN. I THINK I, UM, LOST MY . . . D-DIARY!!

YOU LOST YOUR DIARY?!

I could NOT believe Chloe and Zoey just screamed it out loud in front of the ENTIRE gym class like that!

EVERYONE heard it and started staring at us.

"SHHHHHHHHHHHHHH!!"

I whisper-shouted. "I was hoping to keep it a secret! BTW, did I mention that MacKenzie knows my diary is missing? She's looking for it too."

"Not good!" Chloe said, scrunching up her face like she smelled something really bad.

"Well, girlfriends, I guess that just means WE have to find it before Miss Thang does!" Zoey said, putting her hands on her hips.

"Yeah! And MacKenzie and her CCPs are no match for the three of us! Right?" Chloe said, giving me jazz hands.

I was so overcome with emotion, I started to choke up right in the middle of my star jumps.

If my diary is anywhere in this school, my BFFs, Chloe and Zoey, are definitely the ones to help me find it.

Maybe things aren't so hopeless after all.

☺!!

NOTE TO SELF

Your diary is a good place to remind yourself that things aren't always as bad as you think. You can use it to plan exciting events and fun activities. Feeling down? Cheer yourself up by throwing a party and inviting all your friends!

HOW TO DORK YOUR DIARY TIP #9

DON'T BE A PARTY POOPER! HAVE FUN CELEBRATING YOU!

Complete the following exercise:

IT'S MY PARTY!!

SURPRISE! You are throwing yourself a really big party because you deserve it.

What kind of party will it be?

☐ costume party   ☑ sleepover

☐ pool party   ☐ dance party

☐ scavenger hunt   ☐ _____

FILL IN THE BLANK

Where will it be located?

My house

What foods will be served?

Pizza

Lemonade

MY PARTY GUEST LIST

FRIENDS

(Make a list of ten friends you'd invite to your
party.)

Jemima

Izzy

Hannah

Olga

Maddie

Milly

Corie

Siya

Thea

Tilly

SPECIAL GUESTS

(Make a list of ten people you'd invite to your party who are alive or dead: people from history; characters from your favourite books, movies, or TV shows; celebrities; sports people; etc.)

Katniss

Einstein

horses

?!

I slumped over my lunch like a zombie. The rotting casserole smell didn't even bother me.

"It's like my diary disappeared into thin air," I muttered. "I have no clue how I lost it. How can I be so dense?"

Zoey squeezed my shoulder sympathetically. "Don't beat yourself up, Nikki. Besides, three heads are better than one. Let's all try to remember if you had it during lunch yesterday. We'll start with the moment we sat down to eat."

"Hmmm." Chloe scratched her head, crossed her eyes and clicked her tongue. She only did this when she was really deep in thought. I could almost hear the squeaky cogs in her brain turning. "Yesterday at lunch?"

"Well, Zoey opened her apple juice and took a sip. Then I said, 'Nikki, are you going to eat that fry?' And Nikki said, 'I was until you picked it up, sniffed it and asked me if I was going to eat it.' Then I said, 'Thanks for the fry!' Then I asked Zoey if I could have a bite of her mom's famous blueberry muffins, 'cause those things are crazy delicious. And Zoey said—"

"Um, Chloe, how about we just skip all the tiny details?" I said, trying my best to remain calm.

"Well, to be honest, I don't exactly remember whether or not you had your diary with you at lunch yesterday," Chloe admitted. "But I DO remember the time you accidentally threw it in the bin when you dumped your tray."

Zoey's eyes lit up. "Wow! Chloe has a good point. If it happened once, it could happen again. Nikki, maybe . . . you tossed it!"

"OMG! You guys think I threw my diary away?! What if I DID?!" I groaned.

MY DIARY?!

ME, ACCIDENTALLY THROWING
AWAY MY DIARY AT LUNCH??!!

That's when I jumped up from the table.

"Come on, guys, we only have thirteen minutes before lunch is over."

"Where are we going?" Chloe asked.

"To the Dumpster!" I yelled over my shoulder.

"You've got to be kidding me!" Zoey made an *ick* face.

"The good news is that MacKenzie would NEVER think to look there!" I felt hopeful again.

Chloe and I sprinted across the cafeteria towards a back door that led outside as Zoey lagged behind.

"Personally, I don't think MacKenzie wants to read your diary *THAT* badly," Zoey grumped.

As we approached the Dumpster, the stench of three-day-old beef burger and spoiled milk almost knocked me over.

But I was desperate.

So I just gritted my teeth, held my breath, and cautiously peered inside.

"I'm in my happy place! I'm in my happy place! I'm in my happy place!" Zoey chanted as she climbed in.

She was doing one of her goofy meditation exercises, but it was so not working.

"You know this rubbish is crawling with disease-laden bacteria, right?" nagged Zoey. "When I get home, I'm going to take off these clothes and burn them!"

Chloe was already inside, busily digging through the rubbish.

But do you wanna know the really FREAKY part?

She actually seemed to be enjoying it!

ME, CHLOE AND ZOEY SEARCHING
FOR MY DIARY IN THE DUMPSTER

"If my diary is in here, it will probably be
towards the top," I said, swatting at an overly
friendly fly.

Unfortunately, all I could find amid the rotten

food were broken hockey sticks and flat basketballs from gym class, and test papers with big fat red Fs on them. None of them were mine, I swear!

"Hey! Check it out!" Chloe shouted happily.

"OMG! You found my diary?!" I asked excitedly.

"Not yet, but isn't this floppy hat really cute?" She put on the hat and struck a pose. "Now I look like a celebrity!"

"It's nice, but we've got to keep looking," I huffed.

A minute later I heard a high-pitched "SQUEEEE!!" It was Chloe. Again!

"What?! What?!" I asked eagerly.

"OMG! It's the newest issue of *Vampire Hunks Monthly!*"

She held the magazine to her chest and hugged it.

"How could anyone toss this? Finders keepers!"

"Come on, Chloe!" Zoey said, rolling her eyes. "Be serious!"

"I'm searching, already. Sheesh!" Chloe pushed a rubbish bag aside and bent down to pick up something.

"OH. MY. GAWD!" she screeched.

I sighed. "Please tell me it's my diary this time."

"It's a Hug-Me-Harry bear!" She gave the dirty teddy bear a squeeze. "I'm keeping him."

"Just great!" I mumbled, looking at my watch, which was covered in a thick layer of mustard. "Lunch is almost over, and we've barely scratched the surface here. I don't know if I'll EVER find my diary."

I crawled out of the Dumpster.

Defeated. And really, really smelly.

"Hey! I know just what will cheer you up," Chloe cooed in a very annoying, high-pitched baby voice. "How about a big fat HUGGY-WUGGY!"

Then she shoved Dirty Harry right in my face.

I was like, OH. NO. SHE. DIDN'T!!

Chloe must have totally lost her mind.

And Zoey wasn't helping matters by giggling like a hysterical chipmunk.

But since they are my BFFs, I decided NOT to get an attitude about the whole thing.

So . . . I just hugged the stupid bear.

I'm ashamed to actually admit it, but Hug-Me-Harry DID make me feel a little bit better. Once I got past the odour. ☺!!

NOTE TO SELF

Sometimes the most insignificant things can spark the best memories. Save your ticket stub from that fabulous live concert or that blockbuster movie. Keep the hilarious note your BFF passed to you during maths class. Hang on to that cute doodle you did of your crush on the back of your lunch napkin. You can use your diary as a place to keep little things that you cherish.

BRANDON

TREASURE YOUR TRASH.

Find two things that bring back great memories. Tape the first one in the space below.

Now make a note about what you taped on the last
page and how you got it, so you won't ever forget.

<u>Now tape the second item here and write about</u>
<u>it below.</u>

113

Today is turning out to be the longest school day
EVER.

PLEASE, PLEASE, PLEASE

let it end soon.

I don't know how much more I can take.

By the time I got to biology class, it seemed like the
ENTIRE school was gossiping about my lost diary ☹!!
I seriously considered just faking a headache and
going home early.

I tried my best to ignore all the stares and whispers
in the classroom. But it was really hard to do with
MacKenzie sitting across the room gossiping about
me right to my face.

I was in such a grumpy mood, I barely said hi to my
crush, Brandon. Even though he gave me a big smile
and told me he had something important to give me
after class.

Sorry, but the last thing I needed right then was *another* extra-credit project. In spite of the fact that it usually meant us spending an extra hour working together in the lab.

Even though our school has a very strict policy about no phones in class, I watched in utter amazement (and with slight envy) as MacKenzie sat there texting away like there was no tomorrow. All while our teacher, Ms Kincaid, drew diagrams of molecules on the board and droned on and on about the day's massively boring lesson on microbiology.

It was very sad but true: MacKenzie could get away with murder! And everyone at WCD, even the teachers, seemed to just look the other way.

Or so I thought.

"ADP is a molecule formed from ATP by the breaking off of a phosphate group. It results in a release of energy that is used for biological reactions and — Miss Hollister, you seem really busy with your phone while I'm up here in front of the class trying to teach. I hope I'm not disturbing you?"

I could NOT believe our teacher actually said that!

It got so quiet in the room, you could hear a pin drop. Everyone in the class, including the teacher, was staring at MacKenzie.

But girlfriend was so busy texting that she didn't even notice.

Frustrated, Ms Kincaid raised her voice. "Miss Hollister! Would you PLEASE put down your phone! Now!"

Apparently, MacKenzie didn't hear a single word.

Highly irritated, Ms Kincaid walked up and stood right next to her.

But MacKenzie was so absorbed that she kept right on texting.

That's when . . .

OMG! It was SO funny!

MacKenzie almost jumped out of her seat.

And Ms Kincaid actually confiscated her phone.

The entire class cracked up, and for a split second I felt a little sorry for MacKenzie.

But she totally had it coming!

"MacKenzie, you know the rules. We have zero tolerance for phone use in class. I'll return it to you in ten days, AFTER I receive a five-page paper on why phones should not be allowed in class. Do you understand?"

MacKenzie looked like she was going to DIE of embarrassment. "I g-guess so!" she stammered.

"And since your message is SO important you've interrupted our class time, I think it's only fitting that it be shared with ALL of us."

MacKenzie looked absolutely LIVID.

Ms Kincaid squinted at the phone and read the last message aloud.

"From Brady Grayson: No, that's way too risky. I have an early football practice today, but I can give it back to you afterwards. Meet me in the gym at three o'clock."

The class snickered loudly.

With MacKenzie sufficiently mortified, the teacher resumed her lecture.

"Now, where was I? . . . ADP, I think. ADP is a molecule formed from ATP by the breaking off of a phosphate group. . ."

After class was over, I had no intention of sticking around.

"Hey, wait! I want to give you something!" Brandon said, reaching for his bag.

"Actually, I'm supposed to be meeting Chloe and Zoey right now. . ."

"It'll only take a minute. I heard that you lost

your journal. So until you find it, I wanted to give you this. . ."

Brandon handed me a thin, square package wrapped in notebook paper.

I opened it and was supersurprised to see it was a spiral notebook.

"It's nothing fancy. I just had a couple extra ones

lying around in my locker. I figured you'd put it to good use."

I just stared at him, speechless.

It was one of the sweetest gifts anyone has ever given me. Lately.

"Th—thanks, Brandon!" I sputtered, blushing like crazy. "It's a really nice . . . colour! And it has two hundred and fifty-six pages and cost three seventy-nine. I mean, wow!"

He smiled and blushed too. "I'm glad you like it."

"Yeah, I do. A lot!"

"Um, I guess I'll see you tomorrow, then."

"Yep, same here!"

"Bye!"

"Bye! Thanks again!"

I placed the notebook in my backpack and walked out of class.

But in my head I was doing my Snoopy "happy dance".

After which, I had an obligatory attack of RCS (roller-coaster syndrome). OMG! It felt like I had a thousand butterflies fluttering around in my stomach. WHEEEEEEEEEEEE! ☺!!

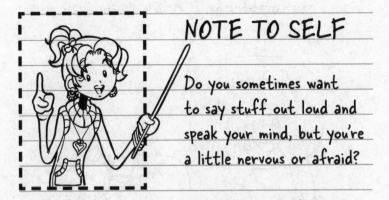

NOTE TO SELF

Do you sometimes want to say stuff out loud and speak your mind, but you're a little nervous or afraid?

Although you don't want to be rude, it can be good to tell people exactly what you think and how you feel. Otherwise, you end up saying it inside your head so no one else hears it but you. And after a while that will get kind of old.

HOW TO DORK YOUR DIARY TIP #11

WRITE DOWN ALL THE STUFF YOU ONLY SAY INSIDE YOUR HEAD.

What are some of the things you've only said inside your head, but that you've thought about saying to:

1. Your BFFs?

2. Someone at school who isn't always supernice to you?

3. Your parents?

4. Your siblings?

5. Your crush?

AAAHHH ☹!!

That was me screaming.

I CANNOT believe I just made a TOTAL FOOL
of myself!!

Chloe, Zoey and I decided to check the lost and
found again between classes.

Mainly because Jessica is an office assistant, and
we wanted to get to it before she did.

When we walked in, we saw two girls sitting on the
floor behind the counter, frantically tossing items
back into the lost and found box.

We were NOT the least bit surprised to see it
was MACKENZIE and JESSICA.

They both seemed a little startled to see us standing there.

MacKenzie quickly grabbed her bag and zipped it up. "Jess, thanks for helping me find . . . my . . . um, lip gloss. I'll see you in class."

Jessica walked up to the counter and gave us her biggest phoney smile. "Hi there. May I help you?"

There was no way I was going to discuss my personal business with HER. "Is Mrs Pearson in?"

"Actually, no. She'll be back from a meeting in about ten minutes. Is there something I can help you with?" she said, glancing at MacKenzie while trying her best not to snicker.

"I hope you haven't lost anything really important," MacKenzie snarled. "You know. Like a diary with a pocket on the cover. Don't waste your time checking the lost and found, because it's definitely NOT here! Right, Jessica?"

Chloe, Zoey and I could NOT believe she actually said that to our faces.

There was now no doubt whatsoever in my mind that MacKenzie had found my diary. I was sure it was probably stuffed in her bag.

"MacKenzie, I want my diary back," I said, looking right into her beady little eyes.

"Yeah! Hand it over!" Chloe huffed.

"Right NOW!" Zoey growled.

MacKenzie just flipped her hair and glared at us.

I DON'T HAVE THE SLIGHTEST IDEA WHAT
YOU LOSERS ARE TALKING ABOUT. IT MUST
BE TIME FOR YOUR MEDS!

But I had a feeling in my gut that she was lying.

"It doesn't belong to you, so give it back," I
demanded.

"Well, maybe I have it. Or maybe I don't! You'll never—"

MacKenzie stopped midsentence, distracted by something behind us. Her frown quickly melted into a dazzling — but very fake — smile.

I turned around just as Principal Winston came striding into the office. "Good afternoon, girls!" he said.

"Oh, my! Look at the time. Got to run! See you in geometry, Nikki." MacKenzie grabbed her bag and nervously bolted for the door.

I traded glances with Chloe and Zoey. They quickly stepped in front of her, blocking her path so she couldn't leave.

MacKenzie shot them both a dirty look, but it was too late.

I took a deep breath. "Hi, Principal Winston. I was wondering if you could help us with a small problem?"

He stopped and adjusted his glasses. "Sure! Now, what seems to be the trouble?"

MacKenzie fluttered her eyelashes innocently and tried to take control of the situation. "Actually, Principal Winston, the problem is that Nikki here seems to think I have a book that belongs to her."

"I don't think it. I KNOW it!" I snapped.

MacKenzie sniffed and pretended to be on the verge of tears. "I was just telling her that I don't have her stupid diary. But she doesn't believe me. I have no idea why she would say such a mean thing about me after I've been so nice to her and gave her all that free fashion advice. And just look at her, Principal Winston. She really needs it. Our mascot, Larry the Lizard, has a better wardrobe than she does—"

"Then how did you even know my diary was missing? Or that it has a pocket on the cover?" I demanded.

Everyone in the room, including Principal Winston, just stared at her, waiting for her answer.

MacKenzie bit her lip and started to squirm.

"Well, actually . . . um, the whole school knows. Chloe and Zoey announced it during gym. And you write in it every single day. That's how I know it has a pocket on the cover. But I swear! I don't have it!"

"These types of allegations will not be taken lightly," Principal Winston said sternly, and folded his arms. "I hope you girls can work this out, because if I get involved. . ."

MacKenzie's face flushed, and she glanced at her bag.

"Okay, Nikki! If you don't believe me, go ahead! Check my bag!" Then she sniffed and blinked back more phoney tears for dramatic effect.

She removed four tubes of lip gloss, Tic Tacs and a brush from her bag and placed them on the counter.

Then she closed her eyes and held out her bag like she was surrendering her new puppy to an unusually cruel dog catcher.

MACKENZIE'S BAG WAS EMPTY!

All I could do was stare in complete shock.

What had that girl done with my DIARY?!

"Thank you, Miss Hollister!" Principal Winston said approvingly. "I'm VERY impressed with your integrity."

But I was totally baffled! How had she tricked me like that?

"WELL. . . ?!" Winston glared at me and began drumming his fingers impatiently.

"Um, I guess sh-she doesn't have my d-diary after all," I muttered.

I felt so embarrassed. I wanted to grab the office rubbish bin and wear it to cover up the word "IDIOT" that had just been stamped on my forehead.

Chloe, Zoey and I traded nervous glances.

"Well, Miss Maxwell, I think you owe Miss Hollister an apology," Winston said as MacKenzie smiled like a little angel who had just earned her wings.

I was so angry I wanted to . . . SPIT!

It took every ounce of my willpower not to slap that SMUG little SMIRK right off her face!!

I stared down at my feet and tried to swallow the large lump in my throat.

"Um, I—I'm sorry!" I mumbled.

"Huh? What did she say? I couldn't hear her!" MacKenzie whined like a spoiled brat.

"I said, I'm SORRY!"

"Now, Miss Maxwell, I hope you'll think twice before you wrongly accuse someone like this again. Do you understand, young lady?"

I hung my head. "Yes, sir. . ."

Winston glanced at his watch. "Well, girls, I have a conference call in exactly two minutes. I'm glad we were able to resolve this issue to everyone's satisfaction."

Then he strode into his office and closed the door.

As Chloe and Zoey walked me back to my locker,

my head was spinning. "I feel SO stupid! I'm sorry I dragged you guys into this," I muttered.

"Hey, don't worry about it," Zoey said. "We thought MacKenzie had your diary too."

"You have to admit, she WAS acting pretty suspicious," Chloe agreed. "But don't worry, Nikki. I'm sure your diary will turn up when we least expect it."

In spite of everything that had just happened, I still had this nagging feeling in my gut that MacKenzie was not as innocent as she was pretending to be.

And now if my diary ends up plastered all over the girls' toilet walls, Principal Winston will NOT even consider her a suspect.

MacKenzie is going to get away with ruining my life, and there is nothing I can do to stop her.

I really hate to admit it, but she totally set me up. AGAIN!! ☹!!

NOTE TO SELF

It's helpful to have a good memory when keeping a diary so later you can write about all the stuff that happened to you.

OMG! I almost DIED when I saw Brandon in the cereal aisle.
We stared at each other for what felt like forever.
And when we both grabbed the same box of Fruity Pebbles,
he actually smiled at me. I came home in a complete DAZE.
And now that I remember what happened, I realize . . .

...I ACCIDENTALLY LEFT BRIANNA AT THE GROCERY STORE!! AAAHHH!!!

HOW TO DORK YOUR DIARY TIP #12

DON'T FORGET TO REMEMBER.

What did you have for breakfast this morning?

What was the cutest outfit you saw today, and who was wearing it?

What was the last song you listened to?

What was the funniest thing you heard today, and who said it?

_____

_____

_____

_____

_____

_____

_____

_____

_____

_____

Did you dream last night? If so, what did you dream about?

_____

_____

_____

_____

_____

_____

_____

_____

_____

Did you talk to anybody on the phone? What did you talk about?

What was the smartest thing you said all day?

I'm SO upset at MacKenzie, I can barely focus on shelving library books.

I just KNOW she has my diary.

But after that SUPERembarrassing fiasco with Principal Winston, it was quite obvious that MacKenzie wasn't stupid enough to hide my diary in her bag and risk getting caught with it.

But if MacKenzie doesn't have it,

WHO DOES ☹?!!

I'm SO thoroughly confused! I feel like I am drowning in a tidal wave of hopelessness.

Just the thought of my diary being passed around and read by everyone like the latest edition of the school newspaper makes me feel sick to my stomach.

WHO WANTS TO READ NIKKI MAXWELL'S DIARY?!
GET YOUR FREE COPY RIGHT HERE!

Blinking back tears, I sighed and stared out of the
library window. Since our football team has a game
tomorrow, they were on the field practising.

I wondered how many of them would read my

diary and then go out of their way to make my life miserable. Lunchtime tomorrow is going to be unbearable!

I was pretty sure Brady, our star quarterback, would be the ringleader. Not only has he been crushing on MacKenzie lately, but she got busted in biology texting him and—

That's when it hit me like a ton of bricks!

"OMG! OMG! CHLOE! ZOEY! I THINK I KNOW WHO HAS MY DIARY. . . !!!"

IN THE HALL OUTSIDE THE
BOYS' LOCKER ROOM, 2:45 P.M.

<u>NO WAY!</u> I COULDN'T possibly do this!

<u>WHY?!</u> Because someone could end up DEAD, that's why.

<u>Namely</u> . . . ME ☹!!

Chloe and Zoey came up with their CRAZIEST scheme yet. And I knew for sure that:

1. Their plan would NEVER work.

2. We were going to get caught.

3. We were going to get suspended from school.

Then my parents are going to

KILL ME ☹!!

And if I'm DEAD, I'll probably NEVER, EVER find my diary!

The three of us had toilet passes, so we were SUPPOSED to be in the girls' toilets.

But NOOOOOOO!!!

We were slinking around outside the boys' locker room. Mainly because Chloe, Zoey and I had all come to the unanimous conclusion that my diary was in there.

It HAD to be!

We think MacKenzie gave it to Brady and they were texting each other about it.

Since the football players are now on the field practising, Brady's duffel bag was somewhere in the boys' locker room.

"All we have to do is simply walk inside, find the locker with Brady's duffel bag, and grab your diary!" Zoey whispered so loudly, her voice seemed to be echoing through the halls and into every classroom on this side of the building.

"Are you KA-RAY-ZEE?!!" I hissed back at her. "What if we get caught?!"

"Don't worry!" Chloe assured me. "Just ask yourself what the heroine of your favourite novel would do in this situation."

"Yeah, right!" I muttered. "So where in the world am I supposed to find a prom dress and a pack of shirtless werewolf boys on a Friday afternoon? I'm just saying!"

Chloe rolled her eyes at me.

I really appreciated that Chloe and Zoey were trying to help me find my diary and all. But I have to admit, some days I seriously worry about those two.

"No one has gone in or come out in the last few minutes," Chloe whispered. "I don't think anyone's in there!"

"Listen, guys," I began, "I think we should just go back to the library before we—"

"OKAY! Let's make a run for it!!" Zoey said excitedly.

Before I could say, "What the. . .!!" Chloe and Zoey rushed the boys' locker room door and poked their heads inside.

"OMG! CHLOEEEE!! ZOEEEEY!! NOO!" I scream-whispered at the top of my lungs.

But it was too late. I didn't have any choice but to go after them.

ME, ZOEY AND CHLOE PEEKING INSIDE
THE BOYS' LOCKER ROOM!!

OMG!

I could NOT BELIEVE I was actually in the boys' locker room!! It's a large, square room with lockers along three walls.

It's a lot bigger than the girls' locker room and has an area with a line of those boy-toilet thingies.

Chloe, Zoey and I quickly began searching inside each locker, one after another.

"Hurry!" Zoey yelled over her shoulder. "It's posted by the door that there's a swim team meeting in here in ten minutes, so we don't have much time!"

I fought the overwhelming urge to panic and run out of there screaming.

We had just about made our way around the entire room, with no luck. Then, as I was opening the second-to-last locker, I spotted Brady's name on a duffel bag.

"That good-for-nothing, meathead crook," I muttered, sorting through the stuff in his bag.

I felt a small book underneath a Spider-Man comic.

I couldn't contain my excitement! "Chloe! Zoey! I found it!" I screamed.

They came rushing over and crowded around me.

"You have to be a real slimeball to steal a girl's . . . *Cupcakes for Every Occasion* cookbook?!" I sputtered. I held the book in front of me in shock and disappointment.

On the cover were cupcakes decorated like puppies and kittens. I felt their licorice smiles mocking me.

But there was no time for me to grieve over the fact that my diary was still out there somewhere.

I heard a man's booming voice and heavy footsteps coming towards the locker room door. Did I mention that it's the ONLY locker room door?

My heart skipped a beat. Chloe and Zoey froze.

They looked at me, and then in the direction of the approaching man, with sheer terror in their eyes. There was no way we were going to make it out of there alive.

We stared in horror as a hairy hand pushed the door open halfway . . . and then froze!

". . . What do you mean we have only two buses for the game tomorrow? I specifically ordered THREE buses! How are we supposed to play with only part of our team?! I might as well just cancel! No, I'm NOT cancelling. I said . . . What? Can I hold? You have another call? No! I can't hold! I need my buses!!"

The guy was having a telephone conversation right there in the doorway. And lucky for us, a VERY long one.

That's when I noticed the huge cart of dirty football uniforms and equipment about three metres away.

"Chloe! Zoey!" I whispered, and pointed.

The girls immediately understood my plan. Within seconds the three of us were at that cart.

We grabbed football jerseys, trousers, helmets and shoes, and we dressed faster than we ever had in our entire lives. And just in time!

Coach "Rowdy" Rowling's nostrils flared when he saw us standing there in our football uniforms twiddling our thumbs.

"What the Sam Hill is this?" he shouted. "Why do I have three players in here hangin' around like they're waiting for the city bus? What's your excuse, Clayton?"

He pointed at Zoey, who was wearing a jersey that said "Clayton" on the back. She shook so badly her helmet rattled.

"Answer me! What's wrong, Clayton? Cat got your tongue?"

"M—men are not prisoners of fate, but only prisoners of their own minds," she stuttered. "Franklin D. Roosevelt."

Coach Rowling furrowed his brow and stared at Zoey like she had just answered him in Swedish.

"That doesn't even make sense! You think you're funny? How 'bout y'all doin' twenty laps around the track and then hittin' the showers? Now, THAT'S funny!"

Someone standing outside the locker room door cleared his throat rather loudly. "Excuse me, Coach. . ."

Me, Chloe, Zoey and Coach Rowling turned to see who it was.

Brandon stood in the doorway with his camera around his neck.

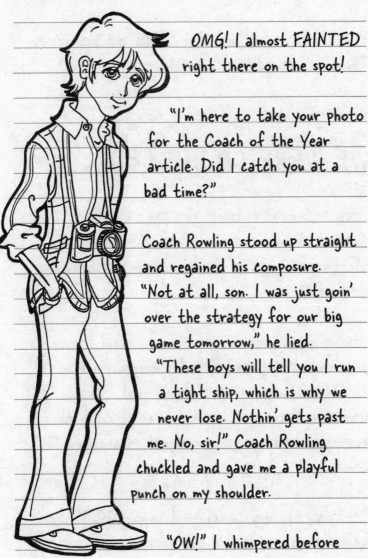

OMG! I almost FAINTED right there on the spot!

"I'm here to take your photo for the Coach of the Year article. Did I catch you at a bad time?"

Coach Rowling stood up straight and regained his composure. "Not at all, son. I was just goin' over the strategy for our big game tomorrow," he lied. "These boys will tell you I run a tight ship, which is why we never lose. Nothin' gets past me. No, sir!" Coach Rowling chuckled and gave me a playful punch on my shoulder.

"OW!" I whimpered before

thinking. "I mean, 'OWW!'" I said in my deepest boyish voice.

Brandon stared at me, then Chloe, and then Zoey for what seemed like forever.

Shaking his head, he blinked in disbelief.

WE WERE SO BUSTED!

"Hey, let's head outside. You can take some pictures of me in action." Coach Rowling did one of those corny poses like he was running the ball downfield.

"Actually . . . would you mind if I steal these guys from practice?" Brandon asked, pointing to Chloe, Zoey and me. "I, um, want to interview them for the article so readers will know just how, um . . . awesome you are as a coach."

"He's only the most awesomest coach EVER!" I croaked in my horrible boy voice.

"He's the man!" grunted Zoey.

"Yeah, bro," added Chloe. "And he lets us do cool guy stuff, like burp. And hit things. And play in the ball pit at Queasy Cheesy and—"

I gave her a hard kick to zip it. Clearly, the only boy Chloe knows is her little brother, Joey.

"Right!" Brandon laughed nervously. "So . . . anyway, Coach, is that cool with you? Once I interview Team Rowling, I can take your photo."

"Team Rowling? I like the sound of that. Take as much time as you need. When you're ready, I'll be out on the field."

Coach Rowling winked and then headed out the door.

We stood in silence until it shut behind him.

"Nikki, Chloe, Zoey! WHAT are you doing dressed like football players in the BOYS' locker room?!" Brandon asked.

"Actually, I can explain." I took off my helmet. "We were looking for my diary. We thought MacKenzie might have given it to Brady. So we decided to check his duffel bag." I hung my head in shame. "But I was wrong. He didn't have it."

"Well, you guys better get out of here! Before Coach remembers those laps and comes looking for you."

"Thanks for saving our skins," Zoey said.

"No problem. I hope you find your diary, Nikki."

Brandon gave me a sincere smile that normally would've made me melt like a Popsicle.

But, given the fact that my life was over, I only mustered a half smile. "Thank you, Brandon. We really appreciate you helping us out of this mess!" I said.

But in my heart I felt all hope was lost.

I didn't want to put my friends or MYSELF through any more drama.

NOTE TO MY FUTURE SELF:

Dear Future Self,

If you're reading this, I've probably been publicly humiliated and banished by MacKenzie to an unknown island in the Pacific.

Even though I am now a freaky hermit person, please

let Brianna know she's still not allowed to go into my room. I hope things worked out for you and Brandon.

Love,
Nikki Maxwell

P.S. Please burn this diary so no one else can read it.

NOTE TO SELF

One of the best parts about a diary is that you can look back at all the silly things you said years, months, weeks, days and even hours ago. It's common to read entries from the past.

But if you think about it, a diary is almost like a time machine to both your past AND your future!

HOW?

You can write an entry to your future self, then come back and read it later!

Weird, huh?

But VERY COOL!

DEAR FUTURE SELF,

BE PEN PALS WITH YOUR FUTURE SELF!

What would you say to the eighteen-year-old version of yourself? Write a letter to your eighteen-year-old self.

Dear Eighteen-Year-Old Me,

Sincerely,

_____-Year-Old Me

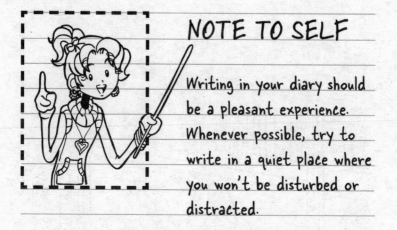

NOTE TO SELF

Writing in your diary should be a pleasant experience. Whenever possible, try to write in a quiet place where you won't be disturbed or distracted.

HOW TO DORK YOUR DIARY TIP #14

FIND A COMFY SPOT AND CHILLAX AS YOU WRITE.

Where would you choose for your secret diary-writing hideout?

ME, IN MY
SECRET
DIARY-WRITING HIDEOUT!

Draw a picture of yourself writing in your diary in your secret hideout.

WHY, WHY, WHY is my life SO horrendously CRUDDY ☹?!

I think my diary is LOST FOREVER.

Especially since MacKenzie is looking for it too.

I would have sworn she had it in her bag in the office, but I guess I was wrong.

I think she was only pretending to have my diary so that I'd give up and stop looking for it. Having me totally out of the picture would've greatly improved her chances of actually finding it.

I know it's kind of complicated. But MacKenzie makes EVERYTHING complicated.

I am so NOT looking forward to having the entire school reading all of my personal business.

But I guess I'll survive it.

Just like I've managed to survive all the other major disasters in my pathetic little life.

Thank goodness my BFFs, Chloe and Zoey, have got my back.

I still can't believe they were willing to risk going into the boys' locker room like that, just to help me find my diary.

They're the best friends EVER!

Right now I'm a bundle of raw nerves and conflicting emotions.

I FEEL HAPPY, ANGRY, RELIEVED AND SUPER-INSECURE ALL AT THE SAME TIME.

WHY?

I was in the middle of throwing a massive pity party for myself when Brianna came rushing in from school, screaming at the top of her lungs.

"Nikki! Nikki! I have very happy news! You'll never guess what happened in school today!"

I was drinking a bottle of water, because throwing a pity party is exhausting work and can make you very hot and thirsty.

ME, TAKING A SHORT BREAK FROM MY PITY PARTY TO DRINK A BOTTLED WATER

"BRIANNA! YOU TOOK MY DIARY TO SCHOOL FOR SHOW-AND-TELL??!!" I screamed.

I was so shocked, I didn't know whether to YELL at her for taking it or THANK her for returning it. But since I no longer had to worry about MacKenzie plastering pages of my diary around the school, it was actually a no-brainer.

I gave my bratty little sister a humongous bear hug!

Then I made Brianna promise to NEVER, EVER touch my stuff again without asking for permission first. Our little ceremony was such a bonding experience for us as sisters, I almost shed a tear. . .

I PROMISE AND PLEDGE
TO NEVER TAKE OR BORROW.

'CAUSE NIKKI WILL BE
SO MAD AT ME,
SHE'LL KNOCK ME INTO TOMORROW!

Of course, being the pathological liar that she is, Brianna totally denied taking my diary.

"Miss Penelope stole your stupid diary, not ME! I told her not to do it, but she didn't even listen to me!"

That was Brianna's story, and she was sticking to it.

Although, now that I think about it, Miss Penelope and MacKenzie have a lot in common:

1. They are both SUPERannoying.

2. They both have a HUGE MOUTH.

3. They both wear WAY too much lip gloss.

4. They both enjoy TORTURING me.

5. They both have NO BRAIN whatsoever.

OMG! They're probably identical twins who were separated at birth!!

But I have to admit, I'm not perfect either.

Seriously, folks . . .

I'M SUCH A DORK ☺!!

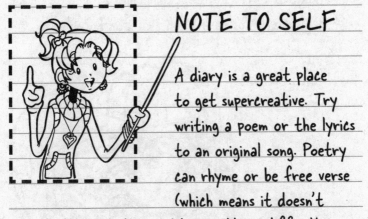

NOTE TO SELF

A diary is a great place to get supercreative. Try writing a poem or the lyrics to an original song. Poetry can rhyme or be free verse (which means it doesn't rhyme). Although this might seem like a difficult or boring task, it's actually EASY and FUN! Think about your favourite rapper or rap song. Rap is just another form of poetry!

HOW TO DORK YOUR DIARY TIP #15

WRITING POETRY IS A SNAP WHEN YOU THINK OF IT AS RAP.

First you're going to need a stage name. You can add "MC" or "LIL" to your own name or make up something silly. Write your rap, poem, or song on the next page. Hey! You're a poet and don't know it.

TITLE OF YOUR POEM

by _____

YOUR STAGE NAME

183

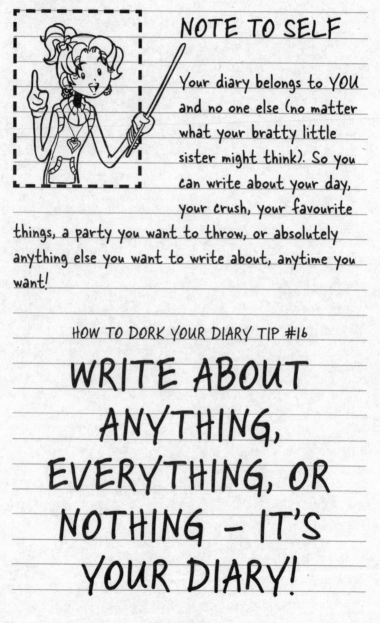

NOTE TO SELF

Your diary belongs to YOU and no one else (no matter what your bratty little sister might think). So you can write about your day, your crush, your favourite things, a party you want to throw, or absolutely anything else you want to write about, anytime you want!

HOW TO DORK YOUR DIARY TIP #16

WRITE ABOUT ANYTHING, EVERYTHING, OR NOTHING – IT'S YOUR DIARY!

Go online for

Visit the **Dork Diaries** webpage

 www. **DORK** *diaries* .com

for extra info on all the books in the **DORK Diaries** series and the author Rachel Renée Russell, as well as a fab widget that lets you create your very own Dork cartoon!

Plus read **Nikki's** blog at

www. **DORK** *diaries* **blog** .com

where she spills extra gossip that you won't find in the books, posts competitions, videos and responds to fans questions and queries.

more dorky fun!

And don't forget to log on to
http://series.simonandschuster.co.uk/dork-diaries
for exclusive video content, activity sheets,
news about the series and much more!

Rachel Renée Russell is an attorney who prefers writing tween books to legal briefs. (Mainly because books are a lot more fun and pajamas and bunny slippers aren't allowed in court.)

She has raised two daughters and lived to tell about it. Her hobbies include growing purple flowers and doing totally useless crafts (like, for example, making a microwave oven out of Popsicle sticks, glue, and glitter). Rachel lives in northern Virginia with a spoiled pet Yorkie who terrorizes her daily by climbing on top of a computer cabinet and pelting her with stuffed animals while she writes. And, yes, Rachel considers herself a total Dork.